STUNTS

BEHIND THE SCENES

WRITTEN BY PAUL ROBINSON

CONTENTS

Words in **BOLD** can be found in the glossary.

DISCLAIMER:

The activities in this book have been performed by people who are experienced professionals, or by people who have had professional training. Neither the publisher nor the author shall be liable for any bodily harm or damage to property whatsoever that may be caused or sustained as a result of conducting any of the activities featured in this book.

INTRODUCTION TO STUNTS

The world of **extreme** sports is made up of lots of different sports. These athletes enjoy trying new stunts and learning to jump, flip, spin, and twist through the air. They never stop looking for new ways to enjoy their sport.

RISKY BUSINESS

Extreme sports mean danger! If you do stunts on bikes, skates, or boards, there is a high risk of getting hurt. Wearing safety gear is always essential.

Starter lessons from experts are a great idea too. They teach the basic skills of the sport so the beginner can learn the best techniques from the start.

TRUE STORY

USA's Mat Hoffman is one of the best BMX riders ever, but success has come at a price. Mat has broken more than 50 bones in his body during his career.

STUNTS IN SPORTS

Extreme sports that showcase stunts are real crowd-pleasers!

THE X GAMES

BMX BIKES

INLINE SKATING

SKATEBOARDING

SNOWBOARDING

THE X GAMES

The X Games – originally "The Extreme Games" – have been held in the USA every year since 1995. Extreme sports athletes from all over the world go to show off their latest moves. They take part in many different events to win **gold**, **silver**, and **bronze** medals.

HOT OR COLD?

The X Games are split into two seasons per year. In summer, competing sports include motocross, mountain biking, BMX, and skateboarding. In winter, competing sports include skiing, snowboarding, and snowmobile events. There are many categories within each sport.

X GAMES RECORDS

Athletes are always trying to break records. The X Games has seen many impressive sights in its history, including:

- BMX: Mike Escamilla completed the longest BMX **360°** ramp jump in 2005, flying 50.5 feet (15.4 m)!
- Skateboarding: Skateboarding legend Tony Hawk completed the world's first two-and-a-half mid-air spin (900°) in 1999.
- Snowboarding: Mark McMorris is the top Winter X Games athlete of all time. He has won 23 medals!

DID YOU KNOW?

Inline skating was once in the X Games, but was removed in 2005 because it wasn't as popular as other sports.

BMX

BMX stands for "Bicycle Motocross". The sport started in California, USA, in the 1970s, when a group of children copied their motocross heroes. In motocross, motorbikes race over mud or sand tracks, jumping hills and twisting around tight bends. The first BMX racers did the same things on bicycles!

BIGGER AND BETTER

While the sport started with normal road bikes, new types of bikes were soon created. These were specially designed for better BMX performance. BMX bikes are smaller and stronger than road bikes, and have shorter **wheelbases**, which makes them perfect for racing or stunts!

BIKE STYLES

There are three kinds of BMX bikes. Athletes choose their bike depending on how they want to ride it.

RACE BMX

These bikes are not designed for tricks; they are light and designed for quick sprints at speed. Races are shorter than 45 seconds long and the riders don't sit down!

FREESTYLE BMX

Freestyle bikes are built to ride ramps, rails, and jumps. Park riding and street riding are where you would see most freestyle bikes in action.

DIRT JUMP BMX

With dirt jumping, the goal is to get big air and do tricks in the best style. These bikes are like a combination of BMX race bikes and mountain bikes. The tires have a thick **tread** to help the bike grip the rough ground.

ACTION IN THE AIR

BMX isn't just about racing around the tracks. Freestyle events are based on athletes doing daring flips, tricks, and stunts! There are two main types of BMX stunts: flatland and vert.

FLATLAND STUNTS

These stunts are done on flat ground and often involve balancing the bike while lifting parts of it off the ground! This includes tricks such as:

ENDO

Where the bike is balanced on the front wheel only.

BUNNYHOP

Where the rider "hops" by pulling the bike up so both wheels leave the ground.

VERT STUNTS

These daring stunts need a ramp so steep it's vertical – that's where the name comes from! This way the rider can get the bike off the ground to perform tricks, like:

CANCAN

Where the rider flips one leg over the bike so that both legs are on the same side.

TABLETOP

Where the rider leaps into the air, then pulls the bike sideways so it lies flat in the air.

DID YOU KNOW?

The first skateparks were only for skateboards. Now some parks and tracks let bikes share the action. The ramps are also ideal for BMX vert stunts.

TRUE STORY

BMX star, Dave Mirra, made history in 2000 by becoming the first person to land a double backflip in the X Games. He came first, winning the gold medal!

DIRT JUMPING

Dirt jumping tracks are made from mounds of mud, and come in different shapes and sizes. BMX riders ride up one mound, fly through the air, then land on another. The trick is to run-up at top speed. This gives the rider enough height to do a mid-air stunt before landing again.

REACHING THE PODIUM

In X Games' BMX dirt jumping contests, riders make runs around a set course, doing lots of tricks and jumps as they go. Athletes compete in rounds, with only the best getting through to the final round, and the best of the best winning.

ALL THE GEAR

Performing stunts, flips, and tricks on BMX bikes can be dangerous, so wearing the right gear is really important. Riders should always wear a helmet, long trousers and a long-sleeved shirt, knee and elbow pads, and enclosed shoes to protect all different parts of their body.

DID YOU KNOW?

The dips between the mounds of earth on dirt jumping courses are called canyons. Riders can be many feet (or meters) above the canyon at the top of their jump!

INLINE SKATING

The first inline skates were made in the 1700s in Holland. They ran on wooden wheels. Today's skates have four or five plastic wheels, all in a straight line.

HOCKEY TRAINING

The first modern inline skates were made by brothers Scott and Brennan Olson from Minneapolis, USA. They played ice hockey, but wanted to train in the summer too. They took the blades off their boots and added wheels and a brake. Later, they formed the company Rollerblade Inc, which has sold millions of pairs of skates all over the world.

INLINE STUNT SKATES

Stunt skates have four small, hard wheels that make them ideal for performing jumps and stunts. Plastic or metal "grind plates" along the sides help to protect the wheels when the skates are used for stunts. This type of skating is often called "aggressive skating".

DID YOU KNOW?

Inline skaters don't just do stunts – they also race! Events can take place on short tracks, where sprinting is key, or longer, distance races where stamina is equally as important as speed! Racing skates are designed differently from stunt skates.

TRUE STORY

The fastest speed reached on inline skates (downhill) is 82 miles per hour (132 km/h), a record held by Gabe Holm from the USA!

BUZZ OF THE BLADES

Like BMX riders, inline skaters are now welcome at some skateparks. They use the ramps to perform many daring stunts. As with other sports, these athletes must spend lots of time practicing their moves to become the best.

THE RAMPS

Inline skaters make good use of the **halfpipe**, vert ramps, and **coping** at skateparks, as well as extra features like handrails and ledges.

THE STUNTS

These impressive stunts are not for the fainthearted!

HEEL OR TOE SLIDE

The skaters must have excellent balance to skate on just their toes or heels! The bravest skaters will attempt this on one foot, with the other completely off the ground!

GRINDS

Skaters use the grind plate on the side of their skates to balance on a ledge, rail, or coping in a classic "grind". They can also slide down rails using the grind plates in a "railslide".

SLALOM

Skaters show off their precision by weaving their skates in and out of cones in "slalom" stunts. The most impressive skaters can do this with speed!

FLIPS AND SPINS

Skaters can use vert ramps to launch high into the air and perform flips and spins! These are some of the most impressive stunts, but they take lots of practice to get right. They are high risk!

DID YOU KNOW?

Brazilian athlete Fabiola da Silva has won more X Games medals for inline stunt skating than any other female skater. She's won eight medals, seven of which are gold!

SKATEBOARDING

Skateboarding began in the USA in the late 1950s and 1960s. When there were no waves at sea, bored surfers began skateboarding – it was like surfing on dry land!

BEST BOARDS

The first boards were usually wider than boards today. Their wheels, made from clay or metal, made them hard to control. Modern boards are made from a wood called maple, which is very flexible, and their wheels are made from a type of plastic called polyurethane.

COMPETITION TIME

The first skateboarding contest was held in 1963. This is when skaters started to invent tricks and flips. Today, skateboarding is popular all over the world, and it's even an Olympic sport! Skateboarding athletes competed at Olympic level for the first time in 2020.

DID YOU KNOW?

The fastest speed achieved on a skateboard (downhill) is more than 90 miles per hour (147 km/h)!

THE SKY IS THE LIMIT

Skateboarders need big air to do some of the more extreme stunts. Skateparks and ramps are necessary to perform and perfect them, and even to create new moves!

WIPEOUT!

No one can get good at a sport without making mistakes here and there. In many sports, a "wipeout" is a fall. Skateboarders are told to try to fall on the fleshy parts of their bodies, rather than on their head, hands, or elbows. Relax and roll – that's the best way to deal with a wipeout!

DID YOU KNOW?

Most skateboarders stand with their left foot at the front of the board. This is called "regular riding". Skateboarders who stand with their right foot at the front of the board are called "goofy skaters"!

TOP MOVE

Skaters must master the ollie before attempting other tricks. During an ollie, the skater jumps into the air, pulling the board with them to make it look like the board is glued to their feet. The ollie was invented by Alan Gelfand in the late 1970s.

SHOWING OFF

The best skateboarders can do incredible things with their boards and bodies! Here are some top stunts:

KICKFLIP

Doing an ollie, but flipping the board around in mid-air before landing back on the ground.

GRIND

Doing an ollie to land on the edge of something, grinding the trucks as you move along.

BOARDSLIDE

Similar to a grind, but instead of grinding the **trucks**, skaters grind the bottom of their board!

NOSESLIDE

Sliding along an obstacle with only the nose end of your board.

SKATEBOARDING GEAR

With skateboarding, skaters can move incredibly fast, and stunts can reach amazing heights. There is no time for fear or holding back. Wearing the right equipment gives skaters confidence while pulling off their best moves and is essential for staying safe.

WRIST GUARDS

Skateboarders often hurt their wrists because they naturally reach out with their hands to stop a fall. Wearing wrist guards helps protect them from sprains, fractures, and dislocations!

PROPER CLOTHING

Skateboarders should wear comfortable clothing. They usually wear straight trousers, not skinny trousers. Cargo style are popular as skaters spend a lot of time in a squatting position on the board. Denim is durable, and can be rolled up or cut off at the ankle.

SENSIBLE SHOES

Wearing the right shoes doesn't just support a skateboarder's feet and ankles; it helps them keep a good grip on the board, which prevents slips and falls. They also need to fit the skateboarder perfectly!

HELMET

The most important piece of gear for many sports, a well-fitting helmet is very important as it helps to protect the skater's head during a fall.

KNEE AND ELBOW PADS

These pads protect some of the most vulnerable parts of the body. They can be hard shells made of plastic on the outside and foam in the middle, or they can be soft shells made entirely of softer, flexible material.

SNOWBOARDING

Snowboards are light and range in length from 3 to 6 feet (90-180 cm), depending on the stunts they are used for. The sport is thought to have developed in the USA, and been inspired by skateboarding, surfing, and skiing.

WHICH BOARD IS BEST?

There are many different shapes and sizes of snowboards, each suited to a different use. Freeride boards are best for twisting and turning down mountain slopes covered in soft snow. Freestyle boards are shorter and more flexible, best for tricks and stunts in the air. Freecarve boards are designed for races, allowing snowboarders to go faster on hard snow.

SNOWY STUNTS

Some of the best snowboarding stunts are performed in freestyle parks which are filled with specially built obstacles, like handrails and halfpipes, just like snow-covered skateparks! Snowboarders slide down one wall to pick up speed. When they hit the top of the opposite wall, they jump and perform their stunts.

Stunts can be dangerous, but they look super cool! Lots of stunts include the following moves:

BOARD GRABS

TWISTS AND FLIPS

BOARDSLIDES

DID YOU KNOW?

Snowboarding has been an Olympic sport since 1998 and is still one of the fastest growing winter sports in the world.

DANGER IN THE SNOW

Snowboard parks are good places to learn new tricks. But freeriders want to test their skills in wild mountain areas. They speed down the slopes, flying over humps and ledges in the snow. These real-life stunts are a thrill, but there are dangers too...

THRILLS AND SKILLS

Snowboarders need the skills to swerve away from trees, big rocks, and steep cliffs. They must always be on the lookout for dangers to give themselves enough time to react.

AVALANCHES

Snowboarders fear avalanches – when a huge amount of snow slides down a mountain, covering everything in its path. Avalanches can be deadly, moving up to 200 miles per hour (300 km/h). Snowboarders can accidentally start avalanches by riding in dangerous areas, so they must learn to identify conditions that are safe to ride in.

SAFETY FIRST

Snowboard safety gear includes a helmet, back protector, wrist guards, knee pads, goggles, gloves, snowboard boots, **avalanche airbag**, and a cell phone.

DID YOU KNOW?

Getting buried under an avalanche is serious and many people every year lose their lives. The biggest dangers are not being able to breathe, being hurt from the crushing snow, and being frozen.

RECORD BREAKERS

The history books of extreme sports are filled with amazing record breakers. Here are just a few of the talented people who have done impressive things and changed the way people think about these sports.

HIGHEST OLLIE

The world record for the highest ollie is held by Aldrin Garcia who, in 2011, reached 45 inches (1.14 m) above the ground during an Ollie Challenge in the USA.

MOST SYNCHRONIZED TRICKS

Sisters Naemi and Alena Stump from Switzerland hold the record for the most **synchronized** tricks on inline skates in one minute, with a total of 21 tricks!

MOST BMX STEAMROLLER SPINS

In 2024, Chris Böhm did 70 BMX steamroller spins in a minute, making a new world record! This stunt involves the athlete spinning the bike's frame underneath them while balancing on parts of the wheel.

YOUNGEST X GAMES MEDALIST

Mia Kretzer was 9 years old when she won a gold medal in the Women's Skateboard Vert Best Trick in 2024, making her the youngest female X Games medalist ever.

WHAT IT TAKES TO BE THE BEST

It takes lots of mental and physical strength, training, and dedication to break a world record in any extreme sport. Depending on the type of record, people don't always break it on their first attempt. Once the record is broken, they also have to hold onto it! This means defending your record if someone else breaks it.

GLOSSARY

360° – a full circle.

Avalanche airbag – a bag that snow sports athletes and mountaineers wear on their backs. They can be inflated by pulling a cord. The air-filled bag helps lift the person, making them less likely to become buried during an avalanche.

BMX – bicycle motocross; a type of extreme sport and a category of bikes.

Bronze (medal) – the color of the medal awarded to a person or a team who wins third prize in a competition.

Coping – metal trim at the top of a wall in a skatepark.

Extreme – something that is pushed as far as it can go.

Gold (medal) – the color of the medal awarded to a person or a team who wins first prize in a competition.

Halfpipe – a ramp that is shaped like a pipe cut in half lengthways, similar to the letter U.

Silver (medal) – the color of the medal awarded to a person or a team who wins second prize in a competition.

Snowboard parks – an outdoor area where snowboarders can try out stunts and tricks. They are like skateparks as they contain ramps and obstacles for athletes to navigate.

Synchronized – when two or more things are done at exactly the same time.

Tread – the pattern of ridges and grooves on the outer edge of a tire. Tires with more tread have better grip on the ground.

Trucks – on a skateboard, the trucks are the metal parts that fix the wheels to the board.

Wheelbases – the distance between the front and back wheels of a vehicle.

INDEX

HUNGRY TOMATO

First published in 2026 by Hungry Tomato Ltd
F15, Old Bakery Studios, Blewetts Wharf, Malpas Road, Truro, Cornwall,
TR1 1QH, UK.

A CIP catalog record for this book is available from the British Library.

ISBN 9781835694312

Manufactured in the USA

Discover more at
www.hungrytomato.com

Picture Credits
(abbreviations: t = top; b = bottom; m = middle; l = left; r = right; bg = background)

Shutterstock: A.RICARDO 5bl, 18-19bg; Artur Didyk 20m; Cavan-Images 13b; Christian Bertrand 7b; Denis Radovanovic 2-23bg; Dmytro Vietrov 1bg, 26m; Flystock 24m; 25mr, 25bl; homydesign 8bg, 9ml, 9tr, 12m; hurricanehank 11ml, 16br, 17tr, 21mr, 21bl, 21br, 31b; Juan Camilo Bernal 6m; Jose L Vilchez 10bl; Jordi Mora 14-15bg; Marcus Placidus 27m; Martin Charles Hatch 4b; Maxim Blinkov 25ml; mezzotint 28-29bg; Mikel Taboada 5tm, 10br; mimagephotography 32bl; Nomad_Soul 16ml; PeopleImages.com - Yuri A 9br, 17ml; Sergii Kumer 5tr; shinobi 1mr; YanLev Alexey 21ml; Yeongsik Im 14br.

Every effort has been made to trace the copyright holders and we apologize in advance for any unintentional omissions. We would be pleased to insert the appropriate credit in any subsequent edition of this publication.